A HEART THAT
SINGS *For*
*J*ESUS

A HEART THAT SINGS *For* *J*ESUS

JULIANA MELISSA LESHER

MDIV, PHD

XULON PRESS

Xulon Press
2301 Lucien Way #415
Maitland, FL 32751
407.339.4217
www.xulonpress.com

Paperback ISBN-13: 978-1-66285-591-7
Ebook ISBN-13: 978-1-66285-592-4

Dedication

This book of God's amazing grace in my life is dedicated to my Lord and Savior, Jesus Christ.

"If anyone speaks, they should do so as one who speaks the very words of God. If anyone serves, they should do so with the strength God provides, so that in all things God may be praised through Jesus Christ. To him be the glory and the power for ever and ever. Amen."

—1 Peter 4:11 NIV[1]

With a song of praise for Jesus in my heart,
Juliana

Introduction

In praying about the title of my life story, I believe the Holy Spirit led me to choose the title *A Heart That Sings For Jesus*. From childhood, I've found myself not only talking to Jesus when I needed encouragement but also singing to give me the strength to get through various difficulties. For me, "living with a heart that sings for Jesus" is to live with the blessed assurance that whatever my current circumstances, I am living in the time, place, and manner that God purposefully wills for me in that moment. This peace that passes understanding and unexplainable joy comes when I affirm that I am in the center of God's will, and home for me is living in the center of God's will. When I encourage other people to hear from God, I often ask them to consider, "What would make your heart sing for Jesus?" I truly believe our hearts sing when we are residing in the center of God's will and praying as Jesus taught, "Thy will be done, O Lord."

I write this story because I believe stories of God's amazing grace are meant to be shared as testimonies of faith, which affirm my belief that a sovereign Lord uses broken, flawed people to achieve the purposeful will of our God. A favored activity of mine from childhood has been reading Bible stories of the heroes and heroines of faith and reading biographies of heroes and heroines of history. Somehow even as a child, I comprehended that while these biblical and historical heroes and heroines are often seen as bigger than life, I liked best seeing them as ordinary people, just like me, who God chose to use for part of a grand plan beyond the awareness of these common individuals.

The four chapters of my life story are "A Heart That Feels Pain," "A Heart That Knows Struggle," "A Heart That Selflessly Serves," and "A Heart That Gives Thanks." The four chapters of my life story all include moments from childhood, adolescence, young adulthood, and adulthood; as throughout all the periods of my life, there has been a mixture of pain, struggle, service, and gratitude. The intricate beauty of life is that pain, struggle, service, and gratitude often intermingle. There are many very dark moments in my life that I would never ever want to live over again. Yet, I also am aware of how God is redemptive, and I am grateful for the depth of understanding and insightful perspectives, which I have gained from the darkest moments of my life.

A Heart That Feels Pain

"Praise be to the God and Father of our Lord Jesus Christ, the Father of compassion and the God of all comfort, who comforts us in all our troubles, so that we can comfort those in any trouble with the comfort we ourselves receive from God. For just as we share abundantly in the sufferings of Christ, so also our comfort abounds through Christ. If we are distressed, it is for your comfort and salvation; if we are comforted, it is for your comfort, which produces in you patient endurance of the same sufferings we suffer. And our hope for you is firm, because we know that just as you share in our sufferings, so also you share in our comfort."

— 2 Corinthians 1:3–7

1

Emotional Pain

One of my earliest memories occurred in February 1973 when an explosion tragically killed my maternal grandfather, Charles Urmy, after blasts to install a sewer line mistakenly hit the main gas line on the street where my maternal grandparents lived. Investigations would later show that the construction team had not only mis-calculated the location of the gas line but had also used ten times the amount of prescribed dynamite in the blast, which hit the gas line so as to expedite their work. My maternal grandmother, Carrie (Schuler) Urmy, was injured in a fall due to the shock of the blast, hospitalized after the explosion, and spent the next twenty-four years of her life with lasting physical and emotional pain. My mother, Joyce, was prescribed medication to cope with the trauma of the event. My mother's body unexplain-ably reacted to the medication, and she was taken to the hospital with hepatitis due to a medication reaction and nearly died while hospitalized.

Prior to my third birthday, I keenly learned two key foundational truths that would be at the core of my being for the rest of my life. Those beliefs are: (1) Life is filled with trauma, unexplainable suffering, and pain; and (2) Jesus is my best friend...the love of my life, the one who will never leave me, and the one who hears my every cry.

When my maternal grandmother was released from the hospital, my parents, Dennis and Joyce, took my maternal grandmother, who we called "Mom-Mom," into their home. Mom-Mom and I shared a bedroom, so I vividly witnessed how my Mom-Mom was deeply traumatized by the explosion as she screamed at night with nightmares.

The term "post-traumatic stress disorder" (PTSD) was not recognized in 1973. While never diagnosed, I personally diagnosed my maternal grandmother with PTSD when I was in college and taking an introduction to psychology course. My most cherished memory of my Mom-Mom is when she bought me the *Little House on the Prairie* book series, and Mom-Mom, Mom, and I would read these books in the afternoons when I returned from morning kindergarten. I also greatly appreciate how my Mom-Mom sewed doll clothing for my doll house dolls and purchased our family piano when I was in kindergarten.

My Pop-Pop (who was tragically killed in 1973) was an electrician and had made a doll house for my mother with electrical lights. I do have one memory prior to the February 1973 explosion, and it is of seeing the precious doll house with the electric lights and dreaming that, one day, it would be given to me. Of course, that dream and many other dreams ended with the tragic explosion.

When I consider the emotional pain of the explosion from February 1973, I also think of other traumatic events for both my maternal grandmother and paternal grandmother. In 1939, my Mom-Mom struggled in giving birth to her firstborn child Caroline, who was stillborn as a result of the difficult birthing process. While my grandparents were all born in the early 1900s, I am grateful that my Mom-Mom gave birth to her only living child while in her late thirties—my mother, Joyce (Urmy) Lesher.

My paternal grandmother, Catherine (Dundore) Lesher, who I called "Nanna," also struggled in giving birth to her firstborn child, a son, who was born with hydrocephalus and only lived a few hours after birth. While experiencing this first difficult birth process, I am grateful that my Nanna gave birth to her only living child—my father, Dennis Lesher.

My paternal grandfather, Alfred Lesher, while over the draft age, chose to enlist in the United States Army in World War II. While he returned from service in World War II, his drinking resulted in a divorce when my father was a baby. Thus, my Nanna raised my father as a single mother, which I'm sure was challenging for her. Being that my father never spent any time with his father, I have always marveled at how wonderful my father is as my father and with children, especially when he was raised without a father of his own.

My most cherished memory of my Nanna is how she loved to play the piano and enjoyed walking. Her love of piano playing and walking have inspired me in my love of playing the piano and walking outside in nature. I'll write of my other family members in the later chapter, "A Heart That Gives Thanks."

Physical Pain

Having written of how I acquired an early understanding of emotional pain as a child, I also share of my early understandings of physical pain. As a child, I was diagnosed with scoliosis, which is a curvature of the spine. The "S" curvature of my spine caused back pain and noticeable muscle humps on the lower left-side and upper right-side of my back. Thus, I began treatment at Shriner's Children's Hospital in Philadelphia. The orthopedic stated that I needed to be placed in a full-length body brace, which I would be required to wear twenty-three-and-a-half hours a day underneath my clothing, and I would only be permitted to take the body brace off to shower for less than thirty minutes a day. I remember the process of having the body brace made as if it were yesterday. With wearing only a thin, long, sleeveless shirt, two male brace shop technicians molded wet plaster over my body from neck to hips. The cast was left to dry on me and then sawed off my body. From the plaster mold of my body, the heavy-duty full-length body brace was made. I had always been a very thin child and was told that as I would "develop," I could have future body braces made to fit my shape. After that experience, I vowed to keep my thin body and not "develop" to hopefully avoid the body brace-making process again.

For the years prior to my full-length spinal fusion surgery at age fifteen and for two years following the full-length spinal fusion, I wore a body cast twenty-three-and-a-half hours a day for every day other than the weeks I spent flat on my back following my surgeries. With wearing this full-length body cast underneath my clothing for so many years, it distorted my body image and contributed to the restrictive eating behaviors that I had since a child.

Despite the faithful wearing of a body brace, my scoliosis condition worsened to where it was critical with a top curve at a sixty-degree angle and a bottom curve at a seventy-two-degree angle. The curvatures put excessive pressure on my heart and lungs, and a six-hour full-length spinal fusion surgery was required.

At Shriner's Hospital for Crippled and Burned Children, I found myself on a hospital ward with twenty-seven other girls. The months that I spent at Shriner's Hospital deepened my awareness of human suffering as the outburst of cries of pain never stopped on that unit. I still vividly remember the girl in the bed next to me who had both of her legs amputated and daily cried due to the phantom pain in her legs. With Shriner's Hospital in Philadelphia also treating children from Puerto Rico, the cries from those on the ward were often in Spanish.

During my six-hour full-length spinal fusion, my curved spine was stretched, a steel rod was wired and screwed to my original spine, and cadaver bone from a bone bank was wrapped around my original spine and the steel rod. Despite the cries of pain and suffering, a pleasant memory is when the nurses would push our full hospital beds (as we would lay flat in bed) outside to be in the fresh air by Pennypack Park, which surrounded the Shriner's Hospital in Philadelphia at that time period. I remember watching the deer and birds come close to our hospital beds.

Bones take two years to fuse, thus the complete fusion of my three-pronged spine would take two years and require me to be in a full-length body brace until the age seventeen. After three weeks of being flat in bed, I was taken to the brace shop to have a plaster mold made of my shape for the new body brace. This time, when the plaster mold was made, I still had to be kept flat on my back. Thus, I was laid on a metal rod with my head and feet positioned on wooden flats. While lying on a metal rod, wearing only a thin, long, sleeveless shirt, four male brace shop technicians molded wet plaster over my body from neck to hips. The cast was left to dry on me and then sawed off my body. From the plaster mold of my body, the heavy-duty full-length body brace was made. Because I wanted to get up from resting flat in bed and until the heavy-duty full-length body brace could be made from the plaster mold, a temporary plaster brace needed to be made for me. After the first plaster mold was sawed off my body, the process of being laid on a metal rod and having wet plaster molded over my body from neck to hips was done again. This time, after it dried, I wondered how I would be "freed" from the metal rod on which I was positioned as the plaster mold was around it and me together. With a quick jerk and the most excruciating pain that I still vividly remember decades later, the rod was jerked out from under my back as the male brace shop technicians held me and lifted me back onto the hospital gurney. After weeks of being flat on my bed, I remember the challenge of being able to walk again first with the temporary plaster mold and then with the heavy-duty full-length body brace.

At age seventeen, after years of wearing full-length body braces and when I was finally able to no longer be required to live in a full-length body brace, I began swimming for pain management. Swimming has been a most cherished part of my life as it is the time in the day and night when I physically feel the best. Knowing how important swimming is to my ability of managing the pain in my body, I always ensure that there is a place for me to swim whenever I move to a new location.

Missionary Eric Liddell stated that when he ran, he felt God's pleasure.[2] I truly know that when I swim, I feel God's pleasure and so close to my Lord as I pray when swimming. While swimming for decades was something that I would do daily, the coronavirus of 2020 brought a unique personal challenge to me, physically and spiritually.

Coronavirus (or COVID-19) brought various challenges for everyone. One of my key concerns when COVID-19 started was not being able to swim as all non-essential businesses were closed for four months in Washington, DC. I knew my pain level would increase, which it did. Thus, with increased pain, especially at night, it was difficult to sleep at night, which concerned me because I feared that I might not then think as clearly being sleep deprived at a time when I really needed to think clearly in my position as national director of Chaplain Service for the Department of Veterans Affairs.

Various people prayed for me, and I can truly affirm that God's grace certainly was my source of strength each day and night during the four months that I could not swim due to COVID-19. Physically and spiritually, I was reminded that it is the power of God Almighty through Jesus Christ and the indwelling of the Holy Spirit that gives me the physical strength and spiritual stamina for each and every challenge...not swimming, even though swimming is an enjoyed blessing from God.

When businesses began opening with restrictions, God graciously provided a new fitness location 0.2 miles from my apartment, which had a small, endless pool, where a person swims against the water current. Again, I was reminded of how God meets my every need, and I give praise for God's gracious care!

Another physical health challenge that deepened my trust in God were the discoveries of lumps in my breast in 2013, 2020, and 2021. In 2013 and 2020, the breast biopsies I had done were benign. In 2021, the breast biopsy indicated that I had breast cancer. I vividly remember taking the phone call from my physician in August 2021 and hearing the news of my cancer diagnosis. Various things through 2020 and 2021 with the coronavirus pandemic seemed so surreal, and my breast cancer diagnosis added to the feelings of wonder about what God was doing in our lives.

I truly can say that after the initial feelings of shock and wonder about my breast cancer diagnosis, the next emotion that dominated my life was gratitude. I was overwhelmingly grateful for so many things through my breast cancer diagnosis and treatment. I was grateful for outstanding medical care, which discovered the breast cancer after a routine mammogram and breast biopsy, and which was aggressive in treating me with the best treatment option being a double mastectomy with lymph nodes removal to ensure no metastasis. I was grateful for so very many people all across the nation who were fervently praying for my healing. I was so grateful for an amazing God who, time and time again, proved so very faithful and caring for me through the various health challenges of my life. I was truly in awe of how much I had to be grateful for through my experiences with breast cancer.

One of the most challenging aspects was waiting the two weeks after my double mastectomy for the pathology report to indicate if the cancer had metastasized from the study of the removed lymph nodes. This period of waiting provided me with special moments to prayerfully reflect with God about my identity as a beloved daughter of God and about how my Lord really wants me to be spending the moments of my life. It was during this period of intense prayer with my Lord that I realized how the specific things God called me to complete in Washington, DC, as the national director of Veterans Affairs Chaplain Service had been completed by God's grace.

During this time of focused prayer, I also felt the Lord leading me to focus more on being the hands and feet of Jesus for those who deeply struggle and need God's grace. So, I am grateful for the breast cancer, as it caused me to realize that my heart truly sings for Jesus when I am present in the undesirable places of life with broken and hurting people. My focused identity in being God's beloved daughter who directly cares for people in need of the love of Jesus started with my care for my family as I served as the direct care provider for my brother, Dennis Jr., through the surgeries he had on both of his legs to assist him in being able to walk better again. As for my own recovery from breast cancer, I continue to praise Jesus every day that I am "cancer-free" and believe for God to keep me strong as His faithful servant.

A Heart That Knows Struggle

"Your enemy the devil prowls around like a roaring lion looking for someone to devour. Resist him, standing firm in the faith, because you know that the family of believers throughout the world is undergoing the same kind of sufferings. And the God of all grace, who called you to his eternal glory in Christ, after you have suffered a little while, will himself restore you and make you strong, firm and steadfast. To him be the power for ever and ever. Amen."

—1 Peter 5:8–11

Seeking Perfection

Certainly, my life has been filled with a host of struggles. The reality of the devil seeking to kill and destroy my life is very real to me as I keenly believe in spiritual warfare. My earliest memories are of wanting to be a good little girl who was well behaved, well mannered, kind, and courteous. Into this mix of being "good" entered the desire, then quest, and ultimately deadly struggle to be perfect. I can't remember ever being told to be "perfect," yet I remember memorizing, "Be perfect, therefore, as your heavenly Father is perfect," (Matthew 5:48) when I was eight years old and making this my passionate pursuit.

So, what did being perfect look like for me as an eight-year-old? For me, the perfectionism track characterized itself by a whole host of rigid rules, a militaristic daily schedule, a Spartan diet, and strict discipline for any slight shortcoming. I remember meticulously writing a grueling daily schedule that included rising every day at 5 am, exercising for sixty minutes a day, household chores to ensure I kept everything precisely in order, preparing special meals for my family members, hours of schoolwork to ensure letter-perfect grades, reading every food label to count calories, and never permitting more than six or seven hours of sleep as there was so much work to always be done. My quest was to be a perfect superhuman.

Of course, I never could meet the perfectionistic superhuman standards that I held for myself. So, I always felt ashamed, worthless, and a miserable subhuman. When I felt subhuman, I felt unworthy of basic life necessities and even life itself. This sense of worthlessness would lead me to erase written schoolwork assignments until there were holes in the paper, and I'd need to start all over. The sense of wanting to disappear and erase myself also led to extremely microscopic handwriting in elementary school. Looking back on how I wrote microscopically as a child and repeatedly erased the slightest imperfect letter, I believe these behaviors were tied to my wanting to disappear by erasing myself through anorexic self-starvation.

I was abusive of myself in other means as well such as pulling out my eyelashes with nervous tension. For me, it has taken decades to accept being human and being able to "let go" of the rigid, militaristic, restrictive, and strict lifestyle that I imposed on myself as a child. The reality for me has been a continually fight against the taunting voices of self-condemnation and the harsh voices that tell me to deny myself any pleasure.

When I was in my late twenties, I read a book by Dr. Peggy Claude-Pierre in which she identified confirmed negativity condition (CNC) as the basis of eating disorders. According to Claude-Pierre, someone who suffers with confirmed negativity condition struggles against a tyrannical internal voice that is hyper-critical, abusive, and self-destructive.[3] Reading this book inspired me to intentionally fight back against the self-condemning voices that pounded my mind by intentionally seeking to quote a life-affirming biblical scripture of God's love for me every time an abusive inner voice sought to destroy me. The messages we feed ourselves are so powerful, and my purposeful intentionality in fighting against the hyper-critical inner voices that sought to destroy me has made a victorious difference in my life over the past twenty-plus years.

At the age of fourteen, I was hospitalized for the first time in a mental health unit. Wearing a full-length body brace underneath my clothing because of my scoliosis condition, people would not immediately notice how deathly thin I was as a child and teenager. Not until my hair would begin to fall out from lack of nutrition, my eyes sink into my emaciated face, and I would collapse from malnutrition would the lethal reality of my condition result in hospitalization.

My life was characterized by rigid, harsh rules that I had created. So, when I was given the strict anorexia protocol treatment plan which denied all visitors, all phone calls, my own clothing, and being restricted to a locked unit until I would gain weight, my mind fed on all the additional restrictive measures as I was a "pro" at being self-restrictive. While I realize that the rigid anorexic protocol treatment plans used by mental health facilities in treating anorexia have saved some who struggle with anorexia, which the American Psychiatric Association identifies as the psychiatric condition with the highest mortality rate[4], I can testify that these rigid anorexic protocol treatment plans simply intensified the rigid, militaristic, strict discipline that I impressed upon myself since a child. While I spent many months in mental health units where my weight would increase from a deathly forty-eight pounds to a thin but medically stable eighty pounds, my self-condemning mind never stopped and continually fed messages of being unworthy to me.

Seeking Death

While the rigid rules, militaristic daily schedule, Spartan diet, and strict discipline continued throughout high school and college for me, I was a model "A" student. I was thin as my weight would never go above ninety pounds, yet I was academically successful and did not look like a concentration camp victim. While I had first expressed interest in biblical studies for ministry in college, I agreed to pursue a degree in public relations and journalism, believing that this degree would support my ultimate goal of communicating the gospel of Christ.

Throughout my time at Messiah College, I knew that I was preparing for ministry as sharing God's love with those who are hurting is all that I ever wanted to do from childhood. A highlight from my time in college included a cross culture study/mission to the Navajo Reservation one summer, where I along with the other college students, had opportunities to teach in a Bureau of Indian Affairs (BIA) school. During college, I also enjoyed a mission trip another summer to a poverty-ridden area in Appalachia Kentucky, and working in the college library on the book barcoding project.

From a child, I knew both physical and emotional pain, and I clearly knew mental health struggles. I knew that I was born to share the hope of Christ with those who suffer. Learning from childhood that women are not permitted to be pastors, I had grown to accept that I would share Christ's love outside of the church on the foreign mission field.

During my junior year of college, I became aware of an opportunity to go to Japan to teach conversational English as a missionary following college graduation. Thus, my carefully, calculated plan for ministry was then set on preparing for ministry in Japan. Then, nearing college graduation, came the closed door on my fervent plans of preparation when the mission board made a changed decision, and I was told that I could not serve as a single female.

I was totally devastated as my worst nightmare was true...I was not worthy of being used by God...not good enough to be ministering in the church nor even on the foreign mission field. I felt absolutely worthless, useless, and completely abandoned by God, who had slammed shut all hopes of being a faithful servant.

The tyrannical internal voice of hyper-critical abuse and self-destruction raged within me as I condemned myself for being unusable for God. With the very sad belief of conviction that I was no good for God, I knew the only answer was to end my life. It was May 1992, and I was graduating with the highest honors from

Messiah College, yet I had decided to end my life as my post-college missionary plans had ended. I thought of purchasing over-the-counter pills and overdosing, yet I wanted my death to look as "natural" as possible to not hurt my family. Numerous doctors had countlessly told me how I needed to seriously eat since anorexia has the highest mortality rate of any psychiatric condition. I had my answer on how to die as "naturally" as possible...a death diet of self-starvation. I could achieve this final feat as I had been in vigorous training of how to successfully restrict myself since a child. Thus began the death diet of eating and drinking absolutely nothing and only permitting water to touch my dry lips.

Within months, I collapsed from deathly starvation, weighed forty-eight pounds, had a blood pressure of 30/20, and organ failure. My parents were told that I'd never survive the night in the emergency room as I was nearly dead. By every medical indication, I would clearly die, and there was no chance of survival. While I've had a very strong will since childhood, God's sovereign and gracious will prevails, and God willed for me to live.

As I awoke in the hospital in four-point restraints, I screamed that I could not be held against my will. It was unjust. While anger was all that I could express toward the medical and legal professions who sought to save my life, I now am so grateful that the State of Pennsylvania determined that a twenty-two-year-old did not have the right to end her life in self-starvation.

During the years from 1992 to 1994, I would be repeatedly declared mentally incompetent in a court of law and court-committed to a feeding tube. Because I would fight every life-saving measure, I would also be placed in leather four-point restraints to stop me from trying to pull out the feeding tube and harming myself. In my mind, I had clearly died and gone straight to hell. These were very, very dark years. If my heart sang at all in those years, they were songs of utter despair, bitter agony, and torturous suffering. Along with the strict anorexia protocol treatment plan that denied all visitors, all phone calls, my own clothing, and being locked up until I would gain weight, the added restrictions of being in solitary confinement, tied in leather four-point restraints, and being force-fed on a court-ordered feeding tube were also in place.

Looking back on the decisions that were made by the medical and legal professions about me during these years, I fully acknowledge that I was an extremely difficult patient. During one of my hospitalizations after being hospitalized for four months, I was taken off the feeding tube, brought out of the four-point restraints, permitted to be on the locked unit without one-to-one supervision, and had thirty minute "check-ins." Knowing that the plan was to still keep me locked up and under supervised eating, I made it my sole mission to escape this locked mental health unit.

The tormenting internal voice of hyper-critical abuse and self-destruction screamed all the louder at me that I was clearly now unworthy, damaged goods, and unusable for God. Death was my only option, so I needed to escape this place that kept me alive in a hellish holding place.

As I attentively studied the other people on the unit, I learned that one of the young women was being discharged in three days. I asked to talk to her privately as I had been surveying the unit by looking at escape routes and concluded that the only way out was through the two sets of double locked doors. I decided that I somehow had to be carried out inconspicuously in some package that would leave the locked mental health unit and go through both sets of double locked doors.

In a private conversation with the young woman on the unit, I inquired of the size of her suitcase. We both concluded that I would fit in her suitcase, and she would ask her father to carry the suitcase out of the unit with me in it. We knew we had to precisely plan the timing of her father's arrival.

After my 9 am check-in, I carefully made my way to the room of the young woman who would help me escape. I curled up in her suitcase, and she zipped it close. I didn't care if I suffocated as my death wish was strong. Within minutes, I heard her father arrive. He picked up her suitcase and commented to his daughter about it being heavier than he thought her suitcase might be. I could hear the nurses and the guard at the double set of locked doors wishing the young woman well as she left the unit. I could hear the first set of locked doors open and close shut. Then, I heard the second set of locked doors open and close shut. I was really off the unit, then into the elevator and down to the main lobby. I could then hear that we were outside. Then, I could feel the suitcase set down, and the car begin to move. It was dark in the suitcase, yet after four and a half months, I was no longer on a locked unit.

Inside the suitcase, I remember feeling the car stop. I heard the car doors open and felt the suitcase being carried. Then, I heard a door open. The young woman said something to her father about placing the suitcase in her bedroom. I felt the suitcase be set down. A few minutes later, the young woman began to unzip the suitcase. She then drove me from where she lived in Virginia to a friend of mine in Pennsylvania.

My own experience of escaping from a locked mental health unit has greatly influenced me in the chaplaincy ministry I provided for a year in a prison setting and in various locked mental health units over the years. I have always taken the belief that any inmate and any mental health patient could skillfully design an escape path.

In spring of 1994, I was once again near death and hospitalized to save me from self-starvation. Faced with hearing that a long-term commitment on a permanent feeding tube in the state mental hospital was planned led me to realize that I certainly did not want to spend the rest of my life being forced fed at a locked state mental hospital. Yet, if I was to make a choice to live, I so desperately wanted to spend my life in meaningful ministry for Christ.

Without having purposeful ministry in my life, I didn't want to live. So, I cried out to God, acknowledging that my life was clearly not my own. While I so hated myself, for some remarkable reason, God kept saving my life and would not permit me to die. So, on Easter 1994, while locked on a mental health unit, I made a decision for life. I promised to eat on my own and never try to take my life again with the belief that my life, my love, my hand, my heart, my entire being would be lived for Christ's glory.

My decision was a choice for life—and life more abundantly—which Jesus promises. It was a choice to embrace the entirety of life—the beauty, pain (and I have lived with chronic pain since a child), healing, brokenness, successes, and failures. It was a choice to begin to accept that wholeness is not about human perfection but instead a wholehearted willingness to bring all of me—including the broken, despised places of my being—into a life-giving relationship with Jesus and others. Time and time again, I have experienced how we connect as humans in the broken, shameful, and despised places.

In my recovery from anorexia, I found it interesting to study and learn of anorexia mirables and evangelical anorexia.

Anorexia mirables characterized medieval women who pursued spiritual perfection and believed that the Eucharist of Christ alone was physical sustainment.[5] These women rejected the limited economic and political opportunities available to them, and avoided marriage. They pursued vigorous religious asceticism by self-starvation as a way of imitating the redemptive suffering of Christ. The most extreme forms of anorexia mirabilis involved years of self-starvation unto death, as in the case of Saint Catherine of Siena, who maintained that she could survive by only eating the Eucharist.[6]

Evangelical anorexia emerged as a distinctive religious expression among evangelical Pietist sects in England and New England from the seventeenth through the mid-nineteenth centuries.[7] A childhood of evangelical nurture produced a personality prone to guilt, shame, and a scrupulous conscience. Through private rituals of fasting, believers pursued fervent righteousness in prayer, self-annihilation, and transcendence. In the book, *Religious Melancholy and Protestant Experience in America*, there is a case study from 1830 of a twenty-three-year-old woman named "J." Each time I read this case study, the below quoted statements speak to my heart because it is so similar to my own story as a twenty-three-year-old woman named "J" in 1993.

> Miss J, a single woman from Rome, New York, twenty-three years of age, was

admitted... on March 6, 1830... The patient history indicates an evangelical childhood of exemplary and early piety... She thought she experienced a change of heart when she was between 9 and 10 year of age... Miss J attended worship services and after hearing a sermon on the election of saints, considered herself depraved beyond God's mercy. Her clergyman could not console her. She sought solitude, refused to dress herself, remained in bed, and fasted, telling her family that she felt too unworthy to take food. Miss J was placed in the upper story of the asylum... The staff noted, she groans and sobs continually thinking she is forever cut off from the mercy of God. She remained in this settled despair for the next four months, eating only sparingly because she thought it sinful... Miss J gradually improved... She returned to her father's home, Discharged—Recovered.[8]

I have grieved for others who thought themselves too unworthy to eat and sought righteous perfection through self-starvation. As I've thought of those impacted by anorexia mirables and evangelical anorexia, I have prayed that they came to fully accept the sacrificial death of Jesus Christ on Calvary's cross as the only way in which we can be freed from sin, cleansed, and made perfectly whole. "Having canceled the charge of our legal indebtedness, which stood against us and condemned us; he has taken it away, nailing it to the cross. And having disarmed the powers and authorities, he made a public spectacle of them, triumphing over them by the cross" (Colossians 2:14–16).

A Heart That Selflessly Serves

*"I am the Lord's servant. May your word
to me be fulfilled."*

—*Luke 1:38*

Serving Wherever God Leads

Living with a clear and meaningful purpose of selfless service is something that has been central to my
life from childhood. I was about seven years of age when
I knew that I was called to ministry. My own health challenges with having scoliosis and sharing a bedroom with
a crippled grandmother made me aware of the human
condition of suffering at a very young age. Yet, as a girl,
I was told that women were not permitted to pastor.

I have a vivid memory of one Sunday, after church,
having a conversation with a Sunday school friend. I
remember telling my young friend that we should consider how we could share the love of God with others,
and that I wanted to spend my life sharing the love of

God with people in hurting places—in war-torn areas and places of crisis. I did not know the word "chaplain" at that time. Years later, I realize that what I described to her as someone who shares the love of God with people in hurting places—in war-torn areas and places of crisis is a "chaplain." At that time, we concluded that sharing the love of God with little children, younger than us, who both were the mature age of nine, was what we should do. So, we started a Bible club for little children in my parents' home.

Leading this Bible club each week for four years was likely the greatest joy of my life during those years as I cherished singing beloved Bible songs, sharing Bible stories, helping the children make a Bible-story-themed craft each week, and hosting occasional parties for the little children throughout the year. The memories of the Bible club that I led for children younger than me remain very dear in my heart to this day.

In the chapter on "A Heart That Knows Struggle," I shared of devastating experiences of closed doors for ministry. As I noted, on Easter 1994, while still hospitalized, I made a renewed commitment to choose life and believe that God could use me (the brokenness and all) for Christ's glory. So, in resolving to choose life, I intentionally considered how I could enroll in seminary. Having been raised in the Grace Evangelical Congregational Church and confirmed as a member of the Grace Evangelical Congregational Church at age eleven, I was aware of the

Grace Yoder Scholarship for Master of Divinity studies at Evangelical School of Theology (later Evangelical Seminary) in Myerstown, Pennsylvania.

Grace Yoder had been the organist and choir director (of both the children and adult choirs) from my childhood to my college years when she died. When she died, she left a portion of her unknown wealth to the Grace Evangelical Congregational Church. Some of her estate money was used to create a scholarship for a member of the Grace Evangelical Congregational Church to complete a Master of Divinity degree at Evangelical School of Theology. Not having any money and being hospitalized, I believed this was an open door for me to enroll in the Master of Divinity degree at Evangelical School of Theology, which had never accepted a woman into their Master of Divinity degree program prior to me. I began and completed my Master of Divinity part-time as God had blessed me with a position as the public relations coordinator for Keystone Community Blood Bank, where I worked full-time during seminary.

With the childhood memory of having shared with a friend about how I believed God wanted me to share the love of God with people in hurting places—in war-torn areas and places of crisis, and with the closed doors for ministry in both the church and the mission field, I realized that the federal government would give me an opportunity as an equal opportunity employer. So, I set my heart on being an active duty military chaplain. The government could not deny me the opportunity to minister because I'm a female. I simply wanted someone to accept me to serve, so I didn't care what branch of service. "Simply give me an opportunity" was my plea.

At each recruitment office, I was met with the required physical, which quickly turned into applications for medical waivers due to having a full-length spinal fusion with nerve damage. The firm answer from each recruitment office was, "Ms. Lesher, you will never be active duty." I found myself falling back into depression and feeling as if every door for service was closed. Yet one recruiter took a moment to say, "Ms. Lesher, while you will never be active duty, I'm a Christian believer. I'm going to share a scripture out of context with you." The scripture he shared was Revelation 3:8, "I know your deeds. See, I have placed before you an open door that no one can shut. I know that you have little strength, yet you have kept my word and have not denied my name".

Around that same time, my brother, Dennis Jr., developed emotional and mental health struggles. I knew that my family needed me to be strong, and thus I resolved that God would open a door for me. A seminary professor then inquired if I had ever heard of clinical pastoral education (CPE). I said, "No." He explained to me about clinical pastoral education, and I completed CPE, realizing that God was sending me back to the hospital ministry, where I had suffered so much during my childhood, teen, and early adult years. My desire to travel the world and "be all that I could be" as a military chaplain would be met by going to those broken places in hospitals that I knew all so very well. Thus, my childhood vision of sharing the love of God with people in hurting places—in war-torn areas and places of crisis would be fulfilled.

After seminary graduation and a year of prison ministry in Pennsylvania, I moved to Los Angeles, California, to serve as a night trauma chaplain for a level 1 trauma center. Driving my car from Pennsylvania to California, I enjoyed amazing sites in our nation, including Pike's Peak, Garden of the Gods, the Manitou Cliff Dwellings, and the Grand Canyon.

My address during those years in California was Hollywood, and one night after a particularly difficult night in the trauma bay from a gang-related shooting, I wrote in my journal, "Home is living in the center of God's will." That quote has given me great encouragement over the years as I have trusted God to lead and guide and protect me wherever I am.

During my years of ministry in Los Angeles, I learned more about gang warfare than I ever would have imagined. One memorable experience during those years is when a sixteen-year-old girl came to the emergency room and was in labor. Having hidden her pregnancy from family and friends, she was alone at the hospital. At her request, I remained with her through the delivery process. I prayed over her and her baby prior to her consenting to give the baby up for adoption.

Serving Those Who Have Served

With the belief in what Jesus said about, "Greater love has no one than this: to lay down one's life for one's friends" (John 15:13), I was deeply grateful when an opportunity came to serve as a chaplain for the Department of Veteran Affairs. With a heart of gratitude for the selfless sacrifice of Christ for the freedom from sin and death, I am also thankful for all those men and women who have sacrificed on behalf of the freedoms Americans cherish. As I began serving veterans in the Department of Veterans Affairs, I was mindful of what had been shared with me years earlier about an "open door" when I was denied opportunities to serve as a military chaplain.

My ministry to veterans began as a fee-basis chaplain in Madison, Wisconsin. One of the very special ministries at the Madison Veterans Affairs Medical Center was caring for veterans undergoing heart and lung transplants. Veterans and their caregivers from around the nation would come to Madison to await a needed heart or lung transplant. The emotional rollercoaster of waiting for a donor heart or lung was filled with challenges for both the veterans and their caregivers who were required to be present due to the complexities involved in caring for a transplant patient.

Many of the veterans and their caregivers who would await transplants for months and then be in transplant recovery for a few months became part of a very special ministry, which I called Veterans Faith Family Fellowship. One cherished moment was when one heart transplant veteran requested to receive a new spiritual heart when he noted that a physical heart transplant would not make him fully well. His request was to receive Christ and replace his guilt-ridden heart of shame and guilt with a heart of forgiveness and grace from Jesus. It was a very special moment to celebrate this double heart transplant! The story of this veteran receiving a spiritual heart transplant is one of the veteran stories I wrote about in the *God Understands*, series which I authored in 2008. Being asked to write four of the booklets for this series, published by the American Bible Society, has been a cherished blessing in my life as I have seen and heard over the years how the true stories of faith recorded in these booklets along with the Scriptures have encouraged so many people.

Another memorable experience in Madison was when a pregnant veteran requested to enter the residential drug and alcohol program at the Madison VA Medical Center as she knew that would ensure the safety of her unborn baby as she had to remain sober in the treatment program. Special permissions were granted to extend her time in the treatment program beyond the ninety-day period, and during her months in the program, I watched her faith grow and develop. After her healthy baby was born, she requested that I baptize her baby in the chapel of the Madison VA Medical Center, where she could celebrate the gift of life for her child with her veteran brothers and sisters. The baby baptism was a special, encouraging moment for various veterans and family members who celebrated the mercies of God.

The last special memory I'll share from my time at the Madison VA Medical Center is of the evening when a veteran called the hospital operator to speak to a VA chaplain. I was at the hospital and took the phone call in my office. Upon answering the call, the veteran identified himself as being suicidal. I knew the important thing was to keep him talking while alerting police and VA officials to where this veteran may be located. While calmingly engaging the veteran in conversation, I typed messages to VA officials and police to see if there was a way to trace the location of the veteran caller. I kept the veteran talking for a period of ninety minutes until community police were able to enter the motel room where he was located 140 miles away from the Madison VA Medical Center. With gratitude to God and for all the many people who saved my life when I was suicidal, I was grateful to have been used by God in saving this veteran's life.

While I was cherishing the ministry to veterans, being a fee-basis chaplain meant that I had no medical insurance or retirement as I was not an official federal employee. While not looking to leave the Madison VA Medical Center and truly loving the ministry entrusted to me, I received a surprising offer to interview for the spiritual director position at a treatment center for eating disorders and addictions. This position seemed like the dream job as I could minister to those suffering in ways that I knew all so very well. Plus, the treatment center was located in the South, far better than the cold winter climate of Madison, Wisconsin. While I was grateful for the new position offer, my heart was conflicted as I did not feel peace in accepting the position. I fervently sought God in prayer for discernment on what to do. On paper, accepting the full-time position was most logical as it was a secure position and seemed perfectly designed for me. Yet, I felt convicted to stay at the Madison VA Medical Center. It appeared to be the most foolish career decision I could ever make, yet God has a way of using the "foolish things to confound the wise" (1 Corinthians 1:27).

When I was offered a temporary position at the Louisville VA Medical Center, which involved training to be an Association of Clinical Pastoral Education (ACPE) certified educator for the Department of Veteran Affairs, I was saddened to leave the ministry at the Madison VA Medical Center, yet I knew this temporary position with the training program could lead to a permanent position as a certified educator for the Department of Veteran Affairs. So, I moved to Louisville, Kentucky, to serve veterans and become a certified educator.

While training in Louisville, the chief chaplain position for the Fargo Veterans Affairs Medical Center in Fargo, North Dakota, posted a second time on USAJOBS after no one had applied for the first posting. I had been told that the Department of Veteran Affairs would never permanently hire me as a non-veteran, so I was not even looking at USAJOBS. However, Chaplain Jeni Cook at the National VA Chaplain Office spoke with me about the position and noted that if no veteran applied, I possibly would stand a chance on being hired. I applied and simply prayed for God's will. As God willed, no veteran applied for the position, and I was hired after interviewing for the position. Thus, I had the peace that the Department of Veteran Affairs hired me into a permanent position for which no veteran had applied.

When I moved to Fargo, North Dakota, I discontinued my training to become an Association of Clinical Pastoral Education (ACPE) certified educator at that time. Gratefully, I was able to continue this process later when I lived in South Texas and thus became certified.

I was so grateful for a permanent ministry with the Department of Veterans Affairs and learned more of Native American spiritual practices as I had a Native American practitioner on my staff at the Fargo VA. Although, the weather in Fargo, North Dakota, was brutal for my body. In my thirties while in California, I was diagnosed with spinal stenosis and osteoporosis, which limits my ability to stand. Plus, with the metal in my body, the cold weather greatly increased my pain level. I also found that I was spending a good bit of time indoors due to the bitter cold weather, so I looked at PhD programs at Regent University. I was interested in Regent University as the 700 Club of the Christian Broadcasting Network had prayed for me years before when I was near death.

In the process of looking at PhD programs in their School of Divinity, I came across an article on kenotic leadership by Dr. Corné Bekker. The article was about the self-emptying of a leader so the leader can be in a place of humble submission to Christ for divine empowerment. Inspired and intrigued by the concept of kenotic leadership, I began a PhD in Ecclesial Organizational Leadership. In 2016, I graduated with my PhD from Regent University's School of Business and Leadership.

In March 2011, the chief chaplain position at the South Texas Veterans Affairs Healthcare System posted on USAJOBS. Due to the physical pain I was experiencing from the harsh winter weather of Fargo, North Dakota, I applied for the position. I simply prayed for God's will as I was told that the longest any chief chaplain had survived the South Texas VA was eighteen months. South Texas VA Healthcare System was referred to as a "chief chaplain killer," like some churches are referred to as "pastor killers." I knew there were many problems in South Texas, yet I had an overwhelming peace that I would be kept safe in the palm of God's hand like I had been my entire life. I was selected as the chief chaplain for the South Texas VA Healthcare System and moved to San Antonio at the end of June 2011.

Within a couple of weeks of being in the South Texas VA Healthcare System, I keenly noted significant wrong conduct by chaplains on the staff. Thus, I called the Office of the Inspector General (OIG) to report the misconduct. I will not share all the details of the eight-month investigation into the horrific actions of these chaplains other than to say that it was heartbreaking to see deviant behavior that had been covered up and then continually lied about even into the court proceedings that resulted.

During the investigations into the wrongful actions of the chaplains, and while trying to hold the chaplain staff accountable, I spent endless days (and nights) responding to the many, many Unfair Labor Practices (ULPs), Equal Employment Opportunity (EEO) complaints, and Merit System Protection Board (MSPB) legal cases filed by these staff chaplains against me. I also had threats made on my life, my car tires repeatedly sliced, and vandalism to my apartment. For my personal safety, I lived with another VA employee and her family during the most turbulent months when my life was threatened.

In the end (two years later), all of the ULPs, EEOs, and MSPBs were all ruled in my favor and in the favor of the VA for the disciplinary actions and removals of these VA chaplains. Removing permanent federal employees is no easy task, yet I was grateful to have upheld the dignity and nobility of being a federal public servant.

Since childhood, I had this deep conviction that our government employees are to be deeply committed and busy at work for our nation. For example, when I was five years old and my parents took me to Washington,

DC, for the first time, we first went into the Smithsonian National Museum of Natural History. Upon walking into that building and looking up at the large stuffed elephant in the room, I firmly stated, "I did not come here to see a bunch of stuffed animals. I came here to see people busy at work running our nation." I was five when I stated this to my parents...and I likely have not changed much now in my fifties! Over a period of time at South Texas, ten of the twelve staff chaplains at the South Texas VA were either removed or resigned, so I was able to hire, build, and develop an entirely new chaplain staff that had a passionate love for veterans and the Lord and were deeply devoted and committed to service above self.

With a dynamic chaplain staff and the Clinical Pastoral Education (CPE) program at the South Texas VA of fourteen full-time staff members, eight full-time chaplain students, two fee-basis chaplains, and God's abundant grace, we developed amazing clinical chaplaincy programs throughout the South Texas VA Healthcare System. We were passionate about our ministries in the polytrauma center, mental health care, substance abuse treatment, bone marrow transplant, palliative care/hospice, intensive care, surgical care, women's health, and home-based primary care.

One innovative development I also initiated is telechaplaincy, which is where the chaplain provides pastoral care and counseling to a veteran in his or her home by use of the computer through a video/virtual connection between the chaplain and veteran. These video/virtual connections certainly helped us to reach underserved veterans in remote areas who are distant from the VA Medical Center. Plus, when COVID-19 hit in 2020, the ability to provide video/virtual connections between chaplains and veterans was even more valued and expanded.

One of my most memorable moments of how the South Texas VA chaplains used telechaplaincy in ministry is when we provided an end-of-life family reunion for a dying veteran on our hospice unit who was able to virtually connect by video with family members in four different states from his hospital bed. This was a remarkable and very special moment as VA staff from four different VA locations all around the nation ensured that a dying veteran's wish was granted by him being able to "see" family members from across the nation for a joint family reunion of healing. Another memorable moment was virtually video connecting two veteran brothers who had not seen each other in decades. One was a World War II veteran who served in the European Theater, and the other was a World War II veteran who served in the Pacific Theater.

The Department of Veterans Affairs (DVA) has four missions, three of which are most widely known as (1) Veterans Health Administration (VHA) by being the largest integrated health care network in the United States, serving 9 million Veterans; (2) Veterans Benefits Administration (VBA), which helps service members transition back to civilian life with various benefit programs; and (3) National Cemetery Administration (NCA), which provides dignified burial services for veterans and eligible family members.

When the small, rural community of Sutherland Springs, Texas, experienced a tragic church shooting on November 5, 2017, I also became involved in the Veterans Affair's fourth mission of responding to war, terrorism, national emergencies, and natural disasters by not only ensuring service to veterans but also supporting national, state, and local emergency management, public health, safety, and homeland security efforts. When I initially heard of the tragedy at First Baptist Church of Sutherland Springs, I went to our VA chapel to pray. While praying, I received a phone call that our South Texas VA chief of staff was responding to Sutherland Springs to offer care, and I noted that I would go with her. The tragedy at the church was devastating, with twenty-six people shot and killed, along with twenty other people shot and injured. Nine of the twenty-six people killed were children. As the deadliest shooting in an American place of worship, the experience had elements of what I experienced in the gang-related shootings at the trauma center in Los Angeles. Amid a heart-wrenching tragedy, there was again the keen reminder that no human words could respond to the anguish. Instead, the awareness of God's presence in the darkest nights of the soul and the assurance of resurrection hope in Christ would be the only comforting mercies.

Ministering and living in South Texas was truly very meaningful and dear to my heart. Plus, I had moved my brother, Dennis Jr., to San Antonio to live with me and have him work in the kitchen at the South Texas VA Health Care System so that I could provide support for him with finances and medical care. Dennis and I lived across the street from the VA, and our lives revolved around caring for veterans. Thus, when I was asked to consider the position as national director of Veterans Affairs Chaplain Service in May 2018, my immediate response was that my heart was in Texas with ministry to the veterans there and being a caring support for my brother Dennis. When I was asked if I would pray about considering this position, I stated that I would pray. Although, from May to late November 2018, when I received the phone call that I was selected as the national director, I felt like I had been in the garden of Gethsemane for months, praying, "Lord, may this cup be taken from me" (Matthew 26:39). Accepting the cup of suffering meant leaving the ministry and people, whom I loved in South Texas, and being willing to serve at the National level, which I felt the Holy Spirit assure me there would be deep challenges there. Thus, I really struggled to get to the point of surrendering and saying, "Yet not as I will, but as You will" (Matthew 26:39).

My heart truly broke as I accepted the position as national director of Veterans Affairs Chaplain Service. The well-being of my brother Dennis Jr. remained a top priority, and I needed to ensure what was best for his mental and emotional health in accepting the new position. Being keenly aware that stability was best for Dennis with his anxieties, having him remain in San Antonio and establish support for him there clearly seemed best. I had to believe that if God was calling me to serve as the national director, God would also provide the sustaining grace for me each day and the needed care for Dennis each day. The decision to have Dennis remain in San Antonio while I served in this position was definitely the best decision, especially with the civil unrest issues in Washington, DC, during the summer of 2020.

When I was officially sworn into my position as the national director in January 2019, I was keenly aware of the sacred honor with which God had entrusted me as an honorable public servant in our nation and a faithful servant of Christ. I continually uphold the value of kenotic leadership, which empties oneself of one's own interests and prays for the divine empowerment of Christ in wisely leading with keen discernment and devotion that ensures the well-being of all those entrusted to one's care. If we truly begin to grasp what is asked of us as leaders, we assuredly must know that the mission entrusted to us is only fully achieved by an Almighty God. As I take up my cross and follow Christ, I am mindful of how Jesus carries me amid the burdens and blessings of leadership—and I am in reverent awe of an Almighty God!

During my first year as national director, an all-new electronic/virtual education program for new VA chaplains and VA chief chaplains developed and began, which proved most effective and meaningful, especially with the no-travel restrictions of COVID-19 during the second year of my term. Also during my first year, God blessed me with ensuring one hundred VA chaplains were involved in the Departments of Defense and Veterans Affairs Suicide Prevention Conference, with being able to travel for twenty-two weeks of that year to various locations around the nation, with being able to relocate the National VA Chaplain Office from Hampton, Virginia, (where it had been for the previous thirty years) to Veterans Affairs Central Office (VACO) in Washington, DC, for me to directly report to the Under Secretary of Health (USH) for the Department of Veterans Affairs, and in successfully navigating litigations from problematic employees. I was well aware that God was truly at work! During that first year of ministry as national director, I visited the Billy Graham Library in North Carolina and Museum of the Bible in Washington, DC...both of which were very meaningful days for me.

During my second year as national director, God blessed me by having every chaplain service in every VA Medical Center across the nation now directly report to a member of the local VA Executive Leadership

Team (ELT), having VA chaplains change from Title 5 employees (administrative employees) to Title 38-Hybrid employees (clinical employees), and even achieving three new Healthcare Common Procedure Coding System (HCPCS) codes from the Centers for Medicare and Medicaid Services (CMS) for spiritual care by VA chaplains. These three HPCS codes for chaplain spiritual assessment, chaplain counseling of individuals, and chaplain-led spirituality groups recognize that the spiritual well-being and care of veteran patients is a central part of their comprehensive care that meets the needs of body, mind, soul, and spirit.

During my second year as national director, the coronavirus pandemic (known as COVID-19) also impacted our nation and world. With a worldwide pandemic that had not been experienced since the Spanish Flu of 1918, I was again keenly aware that God had placed me in Washington, DC, "for such a time as this" (Esther 4:14).

At Veterans Affairs Central Office (VACO) in Washington, DC, I keenly witnessed and experienced how VA became deeply involved in the Veterans Affair's fourth mission of responding to war, terrorism, national emergencies, and natural disasters by not only ensuring service to veterans but also supporting national, state, and local emergency management, public health, safety, and homeland security efforts. Participating in the Daily COVID-19 meetings and listening to the reports from around the nation made us all aware that we were living in unprecedented and perilous times.

When I was asked to provide a weekly chaplain reflection for the national and regional VA leaders involved in these COVID-19 meetings, I was truly grateful for the opportunity to provide this inspiration for these leaders each week. Also, at the start of dealing with the pandemic in March 2020, I invited any VA Central Office employee to receive a daily inspirational email from me. Over 150 VA Central Office employees responded favorably to receiving the daily inspirational email, which included a Scripture, inspirational quote, and prayer focus. Along with the weekly chaplain reflections and daily inspirational emails, God also blessed me with starting a virtual Bible study for VA Central Office employees who desired to participate, creating a first-ever VA Central Office chapel space for prayer and reflection, and establishing a COVID-19 Employee Remembrance Wall for the many VA employees who died in response to COVID-19. My own family was also personally impacted by COVID-19 when immediate family members were diagnosed with COVID. God's faithfulness for our family was steadfast as they all fully recovered.

Amid dealing with the coronavirus pandemic, civil unrest also broke loose in our nation following the death of a black American man by a white police officer. Being that VA Central Office is across the street from the White House and Lafayette Square, where the Andrew Jackson statue was attempted to be torn down, the VA Central Office experienced vandalism. Thus, for security reasons for several weeks in the month of June 2020, we were told to work from home. Being that my apartment was on 16th Street Northwest in Washington, DC, and I lived very close to VA Central Office and the White House, I was keenly aware of all the protest activity. During these challenging and difficult times that required everyone to wear masks and social distance six feet apart, I appreciated the opportunities to point people to faith in Christ for the myriad of uncertainties in our lives.

On June 17, 2020, I was invited to the White House for the launching of the President's Roadmap to Empower Veterans and End a National Tragedy of Suicide (PREVENTS). Seeing the role of faith and the faith communities in response to suicide prevention is truly most meaningful to me. The event at the White House that day was surreal on various levels as I walked by numerous buildings (shops, restaurants, hotels) that were boarded up to prevent broken windows due to the unrest in the city at that time. Plus, entering the White House grounds not only required security clearance and screenings but also required wearing a mask at all times, having one's temperature taken three different times, and social distancing six feet apart. Again, amid unprecedented and uncertain times, I was truly blessed to sit in the East Room hearing the president speak about the priority of suicide prevention, sitting a row behind the vice president and second lady, and being aware of various presidential cabinet members and other dignitaries in the room.

Other very special occasions during my time as the national director were when I prayed the Invocation at the 2019 Veterans' Day Ceremony at Arlington National Cemetery and greeted Vice President Pence, and when I prayed the Invocation at the 2021 Veterans' Day Ceremony at Arlington National Cemetery, where President Biden also spoke. In August 2018, prior to being selected as the national director, I also had the sacred honor of being involved in an official Wreath Ceremony at the Tomb of the Unknown Soldier. That experience profoundly spoke to me of how God—who knows each of us intimately better than we know ourselves—knows the identity, name, and unique characteristic of who is buried in the Tomb of the Unknown Solider.

Having served as the national director for nearly three years from the beginning of 2019 to the end of 2021, along with the prayerful reflective times with my Lord in 2021 during my breast cancer surgery and treatment, I was keenly aware that God was directing my life back to the focused direct care of hurting people who need the love of Jesus and to be back with my brother, Dennis Jr., to provide supportive care for him. I marveled at how God had amazingly completed all the specific things God placed on my heart to complete for the spiritual well-being of our nation's veterans and for Veteran Affairs Chaplaincy during my time as the national director. I had the peaceful assurance that God was saying to me, "Mission complete. I have other places for your heart to sing for Jesus."

A Heart That Gives Thanks

"You will notice we say 'brother and sister'
round here - It's because we're a family
and these folks are so near; When one has
a heartache we all share the tears, And
rejoice in each victory in this family so
dear. I'm so glad I'm a part of the family
of God. I've been washed in the fountain
cleansed by His blood! Joint heirs with
Jesus as we travel this sod, For I'm part
of the family, the family of God."

—William and Gloria Gaither Song, "The
Family of God"[9]

Lesher Family

For me, "a heart that sings for Jesus" certainly means
that my life is filled with deep gratitude for the abundant blessings of God. I'm most grateful for the loving
family with which God has blessed me. In this section of

the book, I share special memories of each of my immediate family members. With great delight, I share that while I have been identified by titles such as "chaplain" and "doctor," my most cherished title is that of "daughter." Being a daughter of God and a daughter of Dennis and Joyce Lesher is a title I did not have to earn but rather received as a precious gift.

My mother, Joyce Marilyn (Urmy) Lesher, continues to be a faithful source of prayerful encouragement throughout my entire life as her cards and uplifting messages have been my strength. From childhood, she taught me to how pray and the value of Scripture memorization. My mom certainly is credited with being the inspiration for my public speaking as she would faithfully listen to me practice my "speeches" for Show & Tell, starting in kindergarten. With a master's degree in education and having served as a first grade teacher, elementary librarian, Sunday school teacher, Vacation Bible School director/teacher, and Girl Scout leader, she has been a creative source of learning and storytelling.

I have fond memories of the plays my mother led at our church as well, including "Noah's Ark" with the Sunday school children having animal puppets that entered and existed a large ark and also the musical play "Down by the Creek Bank." My mother and I were also active in our church's puppet ministry with my favorite puppet show production being "Antshillvania," which tells the prodigal son story by a family of ants.

I have special memories of strawberry picking, cherry picking, husking corn, and making Pennsylvania Dutch Chow-Chow with my mother. One of my most cherished memories is when my mother drove three members of an "old order" Mennonite family and me to Missouri for the Mennonite family members to visit their "old order" Mennonite family members in Missouri. During our trip, I felt extremely privileged to also visit the Laura Ingalls Wilder Home in Mansfield, Missouri. My mother's love of oil painting is also a precious gift as she has given me her cherished oil paintings of places where we lived and also vacationed.

My father, Dennis Lewis Lesher, also continues to be a devoted source of prayerful encouragement throughout my entire life as his inspiring and loving letters have been my strength. From childhood, he taught me the value of Bible study and worship with our shared joy of piano playing. My dad certainly is credited with being the inspiration for my writing as he would proofread my story writing starting in elementary school. With a master's degree in public school administration and a doctoral degree in Christian education and having served as a fifth grade teacher, elementary school principal, pastor, Christian school principal, Sunday school teacher, and Vacation Bible School teacher, he has been a motivational source of my desire to grow in knowledge and understanding.

I have a very early childhood memory of sledding with my daddy at a park in my first hometown of Denver, Pennsylvania, and feeling protected in his arms. As a child, my father would play the piano while I would sing and dance on our "stage," which was a raised area in our living room/entrance area in our Kutztown home. I have a very fond memory of when my father played the key role in the church play called "The Storytelling Man" about the life of Jesus. One of my most cherished memories is of my father being the keynote speaker at my high school graduation from Gateway Christian School. My father's love of sports, particularly basketball, is also a gift with my own cherished value of swimming.

Growing up in Pennsylvania provided many opportunities for acquiring knowledge of American history as my parents provided my brothers and me with many trips to historical sites filled with enjoyable learning. As educators, my parents would have us create little reports of our trips and write about what we had learned. As a kindergartener, I could tell you about General George Washington at Valley Forge, and as fourth grader, I could tell you about Picket's Charge at Gettysburg.

I have the most wonderful memories of our family trips that have included the following, for which I give thanks. I'm thankful for fond memories of trips to various places in Pennsylvania, including Pennsylvania State History Museum, Pennsylvania State Capitol, Gettysburg Battlefield, Eisenhower Home/Farm, Land of Little

Horses, Fantasyland, Dutch Wonderland, Hershey Park, Dorney Park, Sesame Place, Trexler Game Preserve Zoo, Philadelphia Zoo, Valley Forge, Independence Hall, the Liberty Bell, Betsy Ross House, Franklin Court, National Constitution Center, Franklin Institute, Ephrata Cloisters, Daniel Boone Homestead, Moravian Putz, Allentown Art Museum, Reading Museum, Longwood Gardens, Hawk Mountain, Bushkill Falls, and Sight and Sound Theater.

I'm grateful for special memories of trips to places in New York, including Rockefeller Center, the shows *Annie* and *Really Rosie*, the Statue of Liberty, Ellis Island, the Empire State Building, the Twin Towers, American Museum of Natural History, the United Nations, Fort William Henry, Storytown, Watkins Glen, Boldt Castle, Great Lakes Lock System, and Niagara Falls. I'm thankful for fond memories of the Baltimore Aquarium in Maryland and trips to places in Virginia, which include Williamsburg, Jamestown, Yorktown, Busch Gardens, Monticello, Mount Vernon, Wilson Presidential Library, Shenandoah Caverns, Miss Hampton Cruise, Virginia Beach, Fort Monroe, and Arlington National Cemetery.

I'm grateful for trips to places in Washington, DC, including the US Capitol, the US Supreme Court, the US Library of Congress, the White House, the FBI Building, National Museum of Natural History, National Museum of American History, National Air and Space Museum, National Zoological Park, the US Holocaust Memorial Museum, the Museum of the Bible, the

Washington Monument, the Lincoln Memorial, and the Jefferson Memorial.

I'm thankful for trips to places in Florida, including the Magic Kingdom, Epcot, SeaWorld, Edison Winter Estate, and Naples Beach, and I'm truly thankful for what were nearly yearly beach trips to Ocean City, New Jersey, and a later beach trip to Myrtle Beach, South Carolina.

I'm also thankful for how my parents visited me as ministry took me various places across our great nation, and I'm thankful for the following trips that we took while they visited me. I'm grateful for special memories of trips to places in California, including San Diego Zoo, San Diego Safari Park, SeaWorld, Mission San Diego, Mission San Juan Capistrano, Chinese Theatre in Hollywood, Japanese Garden, Rose Parade Floats, Getty Museum, Reagan Presidential Library, Nixon Presidential Library, Hurst Castle, Catalina Island, Yosemite, Redwood National Park, and Lake Arrowhead.

I'm thankful for special memories of trips to places in Wisconsin, including Wisconsin State Capitol, Madison Zoo, Wisconsin Dells, Circus World Museum, House on the Rock, Milwaukee Public Museum, and Lake Geneva.

I'm grateful for our trip to Cumberland Falls and Lincoln's Birthplace in Kentucky, and trips to places in North Dakota and Minnesota, including the Red River Zoo, Hjemkomst Center and Viking Ship. I'm grateful for our trips to places in Texas, including the Alamo, San Antonio Missions, Towers of the Americas, Institute of Texan Cultures, San Antonio Zoo, SeaWorld, San Antonio Botanical Garden, San Antonio Riverboat, San Antonio Rodeo, National Museum of the Pacific War, Nimitz Museum, Pioneer Museum, George H.W. Bush Presidential Library, Lyndon Johnson Historical Park/Ranch and Boyhood Home, Johnson Presidential Library, Texas State Capitol, Wildflower Seed Farm, Kerrville Museum of Western Art, Briscoe Western Art Museum, San Antonio Art Museum, Corpus Christi Beach, Dallas Botanical Garden, and the Sixth Floor Museum with John F. Kennedy Memorial.

I chose to list all these wonderful places that I've enjoyed with my family as I have the deepest appreciation and love for our beloved United States of America. I have cherished every place that I have traveled and lived across this nation. I am thankful for her people and the uniqueness of each and every place.

My brother, Dennis Lewis Lesher Jr. (Denny), is a gentle reminder of the priceless value of being a kind, grateful, and sweet person. When my brother, Denny, was born, I was two and a half years old. My parents called my brother their "Sweetie." Because I could not say my "s" sound at two and a half years old, I called Denny, "Wheetie." Denny was a faithful childhood playmate as he would follow my lead in playing "Little House on the Prairie" with me on a daily basis.

During nice weather, we would load my dolls in the little red wagon and "cross the prairies" of our backyard.

On cold and rainy days, we would throw a blanket over the table in the playroom and put the rocking horse in front of the covered table. Then I would instruct Denny to use a jump rope as reigns to steer the rocking horse as he sat under the covered table and yelled, "Giddy-up." As Denny called out to the rocking horse, I would attend to my dolls—Mary, Laura, Carrie, and Grace in the covered table, which had become our covered wagon. I also proudly enjoyed my brother's Little League Baseball games, his classical piano concerts, and seeing him play his trombone in the marching band. Denny completed his bachelor's degree in telecommunications with a minor in music performance from Kutztown University.

In 2016, I moved Denny to San Antonio to live with me and have him work in the kitchen at the South Texas VA Health Care System so that I could provide support for him with finances and medical care. I've been so proud of how he devotedly serves our veterans as he worked so very hard as a Nutrition and Food Service employee of the San Antonio Veterans Health Care System, and now as a Nutrition and Food Service employee of the Phoenix Veterans Health Care System.

When living in San Antonio, he also served as a volunteer in the Chaplain Service of the San Antonio Veterans Health Care System. When living in South Texas with Denny, I have fond memories of enjoying Sea World, the San Antonio Zoo, the San Antonio Symphony, Christmas Riverwalk Boat Parade, plays at the Hill Country Pointe

Theatre, Spurs Basketball game, and movies together. Now, I am thankful that Denny and I live in Phoenix, Arizona.

My brother, Michael Charles Lesher, is an encouraging motivation to try new things, take risks, and be adventurous. When my brother, Michael, was born, I was six and a half years old and loved being the caring older sister of now two younger brothers. In both first and second grade, I was absolutely thrilled to take both Denny and Michael for my Show & Tell during each of those school years, as I loved sharing of being the devoted and protective older sister of my two little brothers.

Michael faithfully attended the Children's Bible club, which I started in our home when I was ten, and also followed my direction of our family musical programs for our grandmothers. As with Denny, I proudly enjoyed his Little League Baseball games. When Michael and I both lived in California during the early 2000s, I fondly enjoyed our long hikes at La Jolla Cove, Santa Monica Beach, Mt. Miguel, and Griffith Park. I also have good memories of our visits to Disneyland on Christmas Day 2001 and in July 2005.

Michael completed his bachelor's degree in finance with a minor in philosophy from West Chester University. He also has credentials as a Chartered Financial Analyst (CFA) and Certified Financial Planner (CFP), and serves as vice president/senior investment manager for Merrill Lynch.

In 2010, I was blessed with a sister when Michael married Rowena Cardona Castillo, a loving and talented young lady. Their marriage united our Pennsylvania German culture with Rowena's Filipino culture. Rowena immediately connected with the educational background of our parents as she has a master's degree in education and has served in the Peace Corps, as an elementary private school teacher, and now as an assistant principal for a private school. At their wedding ceremony in Philadelphia and conducting their marriage ceremonial celebration in San Diego, I remember thanking God for life and thinking of all the joy I would have missed if I had succeeded in ending my life after college.

Two of my dearest ministry moments were when I baptized my niece, Naomi Castillo Lesher, on her first birthday in 2015 and when I baptized my second niece, Genevieve Castillo Lesher, on her first birthday in 2017. Having Naomi and Genevieve in my life as the next generation of our family is most cherished by me as I am grateful I can enjoy their childhood with them—including performing dramatic presentations with them, princess dress-up, Easter egg hunts, baking Christmas cookies, and playing at the beach.

While I do not regret the painful struggles of my life as I have seen how blessings have come from the challenging times, my only life regret is that I never had children of my own. If I had been blessed with children, I would have liked the names of Kristiana Priscilla, Nathaniel Stephen,

Graciana Elizabeth, and Alexander Christopher as birth names. Yet, I spend little time on regrets, and look forward to creating many more cherished life memories with my nieces, Naomi and Genevieve.

God also blessed our family with fur babies. In August 1974, on the morning that we were to leave for our annual vacation in Ocean City, New Jersey, we found a mother and father cat with four newborn kittens at our home. We named the father cat Tom, the mother cat Toots, and the kittens—Tiger, Timmy, Tammy, and Tina. We kept Tiger and Timmy and took the other cats to the nearby Mennonite farm. Tiger was my dearly loved orange cat, and I was heartbroken when she died only two years later. Timmy was the beloved cat of Denny and Michael and lived until 1991 when I took him to the veterinarian to be put to sleep as he had developed health issues.

For Easter 1981, when we had a large snowstorm, I received a white baby bunny, which I named Snowy. In 1993, when I was deathly ill, I was given an orange kitten that I named Sunshine in the hopes that Sunshine would encourage me to value life.

In 2011, God once again blessed me with the surprise birth of kittens. Coming home late from work, I discovered an orange cat at my apartment who was in the process of giving birth. I named the mother cat Sunbeam and her three orange kittens—Faith, Hope, and Love. Living in a very small apartment, I could keep only one cat, so I kept Love. I can truly say that Love is a very dear companion and truly precious gift of God for whom I am ever so very, very grateful! She brings me great joy and keenly reminds me of God's loving care for me.

God's Family

At the start of this fourth chapter, I quoted some of the words from the William and Gloria Gaither song, "The Family of God." This was a song my family sang when I was growing up. I fondly remember a "talent night" at our Grace Evangelical Church, where Dad played the piano as Mom, Denny, Michael, and I all sang the song, "Family of God." Thus, in this last section of this fourth chapter, I would like to write about my "family of God" for whom I am most grateful.

Pastor Paul Hauk, who pastored Grace Evangelical Congregational Church while I was a child and early teenager, has truly had the deepest pastoral impact on my life. His passionate love for Christ and people has inspired me throughout my entire life. As our beloved pastor, he threw his heart into everything from preaching the gospel to driving the church bus. I completed my catechetical classes with him and joined the Grace Evangelical Congregational Church under his leadership in April 1981.

In October 2019, I visited Pastor Paul in a retirement community in Carlisle, Pennsylvania. When I visited him and prayed with him, he stated, "It seems our roles have reversed as now you are my pastor." Those words of Pastor Paul referring to me as "his pastor" brought tears to my eyes and have profoundly impacted me as I have struggled with years to fully know if God really accepts women pastors.

In my heart, I continually recognize that I'm, above all, God's beloved daughter simply on the merits of what Christ has done for me, and I am simply a humble servant of Jesus trying to be faithful to Christ's leading by the indwelling of the Holy Spirit. When I wrote to Pastor Paul about how his words of referring to me as "his pastor" were surprising to me as I had always seen him as "my pastor," he wrote the dearest words back to me stating, "Since I have been receiving VA benefits for nearly thirty years, and you are now the chief chaplain of the VA—I do consider you to be my pastor. I am proud and honored to have you as my pastor."

Another person who profoundly impacted me with confidence was my elementary school music teacher from whom I took both piano and voice lessons—Mrs. Donna Shaffer. Her enthusiastic encouragement toward me even equipped me to play Louise, one of the Von Trapp children, in the *Sound of Music* production by Reading Community Players in 1982.

Being elected to serve as the Student Council president during both my eleventh and twelfth years of high school at Gateway Christian School, which I attended from the very end of my ninth grade year until high school graduation, are also very dear and precious memories for me. I was passionately devoted to providing a meaningful, engaging, and inspirational event each month from October to May for all the students and faculty from pre-kindergarten to twelfth grade. These very special events included Revival Days (with special Bible lessons for every grade level), Old Fashioned Days (with dress-up in colonial or pioneer clothing and the making of homemade ice cream), Mexican Day (with guest missionary speakers and Mexican foods), Everybody Birthday Parties (with special cakes for every month of the year at those parties), Hay Rides, Spaghetti Supper Fundraisers, and Field Days (with sporting events for every grade level). The other Student Council members who worked with me and the parents who supported us were all incredible as we led these very special events each month during those years.

I previously mentioned my love of reading of heroes and heroines of faith and history. As a child, I always wanted to play historical and biblical events with my dolls, such as Harriett Tubman leading slaves to freedom on the Underground Railroad, Helen Keller with a school for blind and deaf children, Moses crossing the Red Sea, Noah's ark, and the battle of Jericho. This love for history led me to write and perform dramatic monologues on some women of faith during high school and later during seminary. I loved to share of the testimonies of faith of Queen Esther, Mary the mother of Christ, Susanna Wesley, Amy Carmichael, and Corrie Ten Boom.

Being a key speaker at several Christian Women's conferences and sharing testimonies of God's amazing faithfulness is also very dear to my heart. Other special moments include being asked to speak at the American Bible Society Church Leaders Summit in New York City in March 2010, speaking at the American Bible Society staff meeting in Philadelphia in April 2019, preaching at the annual National Conference of the Evangelical Congregational Church in May 2016, and speaking at the Evangelical Seminary Friends Banquet in October 2019. God is truly able to do immeasurably more than we could ever dream or imagine. "Now to him who is able to do immeasurably more than all we ask or imagine, according to his power that is at work within us, to him be glory in the church and in Christ Jesus throughout all generations, for ever and ever! Amen" (Ephesians 3:20–21).

The Veterans Faith Family Fellowships I created and led in Madison, Wisconsin, and San Antonio, Texas, remain my most priceless moments during my time as a chaplain for the Department of Veterans Affairs. Other than the preaching I did in my two seminary preaching classes and during the year of prison ministry in Pennsylvania while finishing seminary, it was the Department of Veteran Affairs that gave me opportunities to preach every Sunday in a worship service as the Department of Veterans Affairs Medical Center chaplains provide faith-specific services of various faith traditions each week for veterans to freely choose to attend or not attend. The name "Veterans Faith Family Fellowship" is intentional as it is for veterans and those who love veterans; it upholds the centrality of our Christian faith as a Christian worship service, affirms the brotherhood and sisterhood of our faith as a family of believers, and provides for a meaningful time of connection and fellowship by the sharing of testimonies of faith.

As I have repeatedly stated, I would not be alive today if it were not for God's incredible grace and the fervent prayers of countless people who prayed for me when I should have died. While I can never name everyone who prayed for me, I express an overwhelming heartfelt gratitude to every person who prayed for me... far too many to count.

Some years after the darkest period of my life, Hettie Turner, a prayer warrior in our Grace Evangelical Congregational Church, told me that as she prayed for me when I was near death, God reminded her of Job and gave her peace by assuring her that God permitted Satan to inflict me in many ways but not kill me. Thus, she had faith to believe that I would not die when I medically should have died. Years later, Raedell Marks, a beloved Sunday school teacher and fervent prayer warrior in our Grace Evangelical Congregational Church, also voiced something similar of how God gave her peace of my recovery when everything looked hopeless for me. The faithful prayers and friendship of Raedell through the years has been so treasured by me.

I am also well aware that it is the dedicated prayers of so many people which continually uphold me in ministry, especially while I served as the national director of Chaplain Service for the Department of Veterans Affairs. I affirm what Oswald Chambers stated in his quote, "Prayer does not fit us for the greater work; prayer is the greater work."[10] I can never name everyone who prayed for me and continues to pray for me. Instead, I give thanks to God for each and every person who has prayed for me and does pray for me...how blessed I am! I also ask for God to graciously bless each person who has faithfully prayed and is praying for me. I'm ever so grateful!

I do want to particularly thank my dear sister in Christ, Kathy (Leiby) Gaul. Kathy and I have been friends since I was age six, and she was age five. This is a lifelong friendship, which is so precious. Although we went to different high schools, colleges, seminaries and have lived very different lives with her primary ministry being a devoted wife and mother and an incredible prayer warrior, we have committed to calling each other and praying with each other every month for decades even as I would continually move all over the United States.

My heart is filled with overwhelming gratitude for my heavenly Father, Jesus, the Holy Spirit, and the many people who have been and are a part of my life. Life is certainly an amazing journey. Something that I share when preaching at a funeral is that life is filled with "hellos" and "goodbyes." For each person that we meet on earth, there is a "hello," and eventually there is a "goodbye." What I love to share at Christian funerals and what makes me smile is that heaven is one eternal "hello." We will never ever say "goodbye" in heaven. What I also deeply believe is that we are not taking anything with us to heaven from this life except our personal relationship with Jesus Christ as Lord and the relationships we share with brothers and sisters in Christ. Our relationship with Christ and our relationships with Christian brothers and sisters is all that lasts for eternity. I think of the Steven Curtis Chapman song, "Long Way Home," and my prayer is that on this "long way home," as many people who I say "hello" to here on earth will be with me on that journey as we go home to Jesus.

Bibliography

Arcelus, J., Mitchell, A., Wales, J., & Nielsen, S. "Mortality Rates in Patients with Anorexia Nervosa and Other Eating Disorders." *Archives of General Psychiatry* 68, no. 7 (2011): 724-731.

Chambers, Oswald. *Prayer: A Holy Occupation*. Grand Rapids, MI: Discovery House Publishers, 2010.

Claude-Pierre, Peggy. *The Secret Language of Eating Disorders*. New York City, NY: Random House Publishing, 1997.

Gaither, Bill & Gloria Gaither. "The Family of God." *In Pure and Simple Gaither*. Van Nuys, CA: Alfred Music Publishing, 2011.

Hamilton, Duncan. *For The Glory*. London, UK: Penguin Books, 2017.

Life Application NIV Study Bible. Wheaton, IL: Tyndale House Publishers, Inc. and Grand Rapids, MI: Zondervan, 1991.

Rubin, Julius. *Religious Melancholy & Protestant Experience in America*. New York City, NY: Oxford University Press, 1994.

Endnotes

[1] All Scripture Passages are from the New International Version of the Bible.

[2] Duncan Hamilton, For The Glory (London, UK: Penguin Books, 2017), 28.

[3] Peggy Claude-Pierre, The Secret Language of Eating Disorders (New York City, NY: Random House Publishing, 1997), 8.

[4] J. Arcelus, A. Mitchell, J. Wales, & S. Nielsen. "Mortality Rates in Patients with Anorexia Nervosa and Other Eating Disorders." Archives of General Psychiatry 68, no. 7 (2011): 724-731.

[5] Julius Rubin, Religious Melancholy & Protestant Experience in America (New York City, NY: Oxford University Press, 1994), 168.

[6] Julius Rubin, Religious Melancholy & Protestant Experience in America (New York City, NY: Oxford University Press, 1994), 167.

[7] Julius Rubin, Religious Melancholy & Protestant Experience in America (New York City, NY: Oxford University Press, 1994), 11.

[8] Julius Rubin, Religious Melancholy & Protestant Experience in America (New York City, NY: Oxford University Press, 1994), 11.

[9] Bill Gaither & Gloria Gaither. "The Family of God." In *Pure and Simple Gaither* (Van Nuys, CA: Alfred Music Publishing, 2011), 10-11.

[10] Oswald Chambers. *Prayer: A Holy Occupation.* (Grand Rapids, MI: Discovery House Publishers, 2010), 61.

CPSIA information can be obtained
at www.ICGtesting.com
Printed in the USA
BVHW030907160922
647213BV00014B/357

9 781662 855917